MICKEY MANTLE
SLUGS IT OUT

MICKEY MANTLE
SLUGS IT OUT

by Julian May

Published by Crestwood House, Inc., Mankato, Minnesota 56001. Published simultaneously in Canada by J. M. Dent and Sons, Ltd. Library of Congress Catalog Card Number: 72-77303. Standard Book Number: 87191-202-3. Text copyright © 1972 by Julian May Dikty. Illustrations copyright © 1972 by Crestwood House, Inc. All rights reserved. No part of this book may be reproduced in any form without written permission from the publisher, except for brief passages included in a review. Printed in the United States of America.

Designed by William Dichtl

Crestwood House, Inc., Mankato, Minn. 56001

PHOTOGRAPHIC CREDITS

MICKEY MANTLE
SLUGS IT OUT

The boy woke up. Christmas morning! Would it be there?

He got out of bed and shivered in the Christmas dawn. His brothers and sister were still asleep. Softly, he tip-toed into the front room where the Christmas tree was.

There was a package. With his name: MICKEY.

He opened it slowly, saw tan leather, and let out a holler that woke everybody up.

It was a full-size professional baseball glove, and it just fit his fourteen-year-old hand. A glove like that cost almost one-third of his father's weekly salary. That meant a lot of scraping in a family as poor as theirs.

"I wanted you to have it," said his father, standing in the doorway. "It'll help you be a great ball player."

Mickey and his father in a picture taken when the boy was about three.

Mickey Mantle had played ball with his father for as long as he could remember. Everybody called his pa "Mutt." Mutt Mantle worked in a lead and zinc mine. In his free time, he played semi-pro baseball. He taught his boy the game.

Even when he was small, Mickey had the makings of a great hitter. Mutt Mantle knew his son was something special. So he made little Mickey into a switch hitter. He pitched right-handed to Mickey and had him bat left-handed. Then Mickey's grandfather, pitching lefty, had the boy bat right-handed.

At first, switch hitting was very hard for Mickey. But he kept at it when Mutt told him it would help him later.

8

A successful catfishing expedition by Mickey *(center)*, his twin brothers Roy *(left)* and Ray, and sister Barbara.

Mutt was right. Mickey became the star of his Pee Wee League team. Nobody else in the league could switch hit. And nobody could hit the ball as far as Mickey. His team won championships all through grade school.

Now he was fourteen, in high school. The school didn't have a baseball team. So Mickey used his brand new glove playing for an American Legion team the next summer.

When fall came, Mickey wanted to go out for football.

"You could hurt yourself," Mutt warned his son.

Mickey begged hard and his father finally let him play. He scrimmaged for just a few weeks. Then his ankle was badly injured.

Since his own home town of Commerce had no baseball team, Mickey played for nearby Miami, Oklahoma. Here he is about 14 years old.

Mickey watched from the stands as Rudy York *(right)* of the Boston Red Sox homered in the tenth inning to break a deadlock and give his team a 3-2 victory. Congratulating him is teammate Bobby Doerr. This was the first game of the 1946 World Series.

Doctors said Mickey had a serious bone disease called osteomyelitis. It could be treated, but not cured.

Mickey spent time in the hospital, then came home on crutches. Mutt tried to cheer him up by taking him to see the two opening games of the 1946 World Series in St. Louis.

As he watched big-league ball for the first time, the boy thought: "I'm not going to be a cripple! I'm going to get well and play baseball."

Mickey Mantle's grip

His ankle got better in the months that followed. It still hurt when he got tired, but he could walk and run as good as ever by springtime.

He played baseball again, and played it well.

Toward the end of his high school days, Mickey became famous as a fearsome hitter. He slugged one ball 400 feet. He hit home runs batting both right- and left-handed. Despite his bad ankle, which still gave him pain, he was a fireball base-runner.

He played shortstop—and here he was less than great. He made a lot of errors. But coaches were glad to put up with it for the sake of his hitting.

Just before Mickey was ready to graduate, a friendly umpire sent him to the Yankee farm team at Joplin, Missouri. Mickey tried out and did well.

12

The farm team manager said, "You look pretty good. Go home now, kid, and we'll think about it."

A big-league scout, Tom Greenwade, came to town. He saw Mickey hit a double batting right-handed, and another batting left-handed. Then it began to rain. Mickey and his father went to sit with Greenwade in his car.

"Your batting is good, Mickey," said the scout. "But your fielding is terrible. You're kind of small, too. Still, the Yankees might be willing to risk signing you to a Class D contract."

The salary wasn't much, but it *was* a professional baseball contract at last. Mutt and Mickey signed it together as raindrops tapped on the car roof.

The camera catches the action of Mickey's swing as he clouts a home run.

Mickey was sent to the Independence, Missouri, team. He was scared and lonely at first, a shy boy from a small town. As he made friends among the young players, his homesickness slowly faded.

Out on the diamond, he did well at bat. But he was so excited that he performed poorly in the field. He could not catch balls that came straight at him. And he threw wildly because he did not take time to judge the distance to his target properly.

His errors didn't hurt the team much, though. Independence won the pennant that year, 1949. When the season was over, Mickey went home to work in the mines with his father. The family needed the money.

The Mantle family plays a friendly card game. From left to right: Roy, Mickey, Mrs. Mantle, brother Larry, Mr. Mantle, Ray.

Mickey wears the Yankee uniform at the rookie school in Phoenix, Arizona.

That fall, Mickey met a girl named Merlyn Johnson. She was pretty and very popular. After their first date she and Mickey began to go steady.

Mickey left home again in spring to attend the Yankee rookie school in Phoenix, Arizona. Once again he was homesick and shy. And he was so broke that he could not even afford a phone call home.

The players in Phoenix didn't seem friendly. Only one, Coach Frank Crosetti, took an interest in the boy.

"Where'd you get that beat-up glove?" he asked Mickey. "No wonder you can't field right. You gotta buy a new one."

Mickey mumbled that he couldn't afford to replace his good old glove.

The next day, Crosetti handed Mickey a brand new glove. But he never admitted that he had bought it himself.

Frank Crosetti (right) coaches three rookies trying for positions with the New York Yankees. He coached for the Yankees from 1947 through 1968, helping guide the team through fifteen World Series. In subsequent years he has coached for the Seattle Pilots and the Minnesota Twins. The rookies are Tom Tresh, Phil Linz, and Jake Gibbs.

Mickey played basketball for a Joplin, Missouri team.

After rookie school, Mickey played with the Joplin, Missouri team. It was Class C, a step up from last season. The Independence manager, Harry Craft, moved up to Joplin, too. He took a close interest in Mickey, and the boy admired him very much.

Harry Craft had taken Mutt's place in training Mickey for big-league ball. The manager also helped Mickey to grow up from an awkward boy into a man.

17

At the age of 18, Mickey already showed the tremendous batting power that would make him a major-league star. He played shortstop for Joplin, but his fielding was hardly in a class with his batting.

Mickey did better and better at the plate. He had huge shoulder muscles that swung the bat with tremendous power. During the 1950 season, Mickey's average was .383. He had 199 hits, 26 home runs, and 136 runs batted in.

But when he struck out or made an error, Mickey would become angry or hang his head and sulk. He could not stand to be less than perfect all the time.

Harry Craft scolded him about this. Mickey promised to do better. But wanting to be tops was a thing that would always be deep inside Mickey Mantle. It would get him into trouble in later life.

Joplin won the pennant in 1950. Mutt Mantle and the family sat proudly in the stands on the day Mickey won Most Valuable Player in the Western Association. He was 18 years old.

An important message arrived. It was from Casey Stengel, the grouchy but brilliant manager of the Yankees. He wanted to see Mickey and had the boy meet the big-league team in St. Louis. Casey saw at once that Mickey was a poor fielder. But at bat . . . why, that boy was major league!

Casey met Mutt Mantle at the World Series game in New York. "You taught your boy good," he said. "I oughta sign you as a coach."

Mutt said, "Mickey's more than good. He's going to be *great*."

And Mickey knew he had to be.

Yankee manager Casey Stengel *(right)* explains major-league facts of life to rookies Bob Wiesler, Gil McDougald, Tom Morgan, Al Robertson, Andy Carey and Mickey Mantle.

Mickey went again to the Phoenix camp. It was there that Mutt's prediction about him began to come true.

Mickey amazed the coaches and writers with his hitting. Newspapers began to have stories about him. Facing big-league pitchers, he finished spring training with a batting average of .402.

Casey Stengel knew the boy would never be a good shortstop. So he moved him to the outfield. Reporters thought Casey was grooming Mickey to take over the outfield spot of Joe DiMaggio, the mighty Yankee Clipper. Joe had said he would probably retire after the 1951 season.

Somebody asked Casey his plans for the boy.

But Casey wouldn't say.

In early 1951, when Mickey came again to the training camp, he was considered one of the hottest prospects in baseball history. Here he shows his switch-hitting stances.

Mickey and his father on the porch of their home in Commerce, Oklahoma.

Mickey traveled with the Yankees on their spring exhibition swing. His leg gave him trouble, but still he seemed the fastest runner that the majors had seen for years. His fielding improved now that he was in the outfield with more time to watch for the ball.

When he made mistakes, Casey Stengel corrected him patiently. This surprised Mickey. Casey was well known for snarling at rookies.

At the end of the tour, Mickey said, "Mr. Stengel, when you send me back to the minors, I'd like to go to Harry Craft's team."

Casey said, "How'd you like to stay with the Yankees?"

Mickey could not speak. From Class C to the Yankees!

It was a miracle, and it had happened to him.

Mickey connects for a base hit. During the early part of his career, he wore the number 6. Later, he acquired the number 7.

Even before his first game, Mickey was famous. Writers called him the new DiMaggio. They compared him to other famous players such as Mel Ott and Ty Cobb.

Mickey set out to do his best. In his first game, against the Boston Red Sox, he got a single and brought a runner home. DiMaggio and Yogi Berra singled, and Mickey came home from second. His team-mates in the dugout cheered.

He made some mistakes in that first game, but the Yanks won, 5-0. And he had helped.

Veteran slugger Joe DiMaggio poses with the rookie who was going to take his place. Joe helped Mickey as the boy tried to adjust to big-league ball.

Joe DiMaggio himself was there beside Mickey in the outfield. Joe did his best to help the boy.

Some of the fans remembered how sportswriters had said that Mickey would take Joe's place. They loved Joe and didn't want him to leave baseball. So when Mickey came up to the plate, they booed him and called him names.

Other fans wanted a home run every time. "Knock it out of the park, Mickey!" they yelled.

Mickey got a good collection of hits during his first weeks in the big leagues. But he also struck out a lot because he tried so hard to slug the ball.

And each time he fanned, the boos rained down.

The team went to Boston. Mickey faced a wise pitcher who threw high and inside, striking him out five times. The boy burned with anger. As he shuffled back from the plate each time, he called himself names. He kicked the water cooler in the dugout.

When the club went to Detroit, Mickey decided he would break the no-hit streak by bunting. But he didn't have a chance to try it. Casey Stengel called him in.

"You need a little more work, kid. You gotta learn about your strike zone. So I'm sending you to Kansas City for awhile. . . ."

Sent down to the minors! It had been a mighty short big-league career.

He was just too inexperienced. Other players told him it was nothing to be ashamed of. But Mickey *was* ashamed. His pride would not let him be less than the best.

The Kansas City team was AAA, tops in the minor leagues. His first time at bat, Mickey dragged a beautiful bunt. To his surprise, the manager was angry. "They sent you here to learn how to hit!" he said. "Never mind bunting."

He tried. He went to the plate 22 times, and struck out 22 times.

"I'm finished," he told himself. "Whatever I had, it's gone now."

He called up his father and asked to be taken home.

Late in 1951 Mickey visited his father *(center)* at the zinc mine. At right is a co-worker, Otte Turner.

When Mutt and Mickey met, the boy had tears in his eyes. He had never felt lower.

"What's all this?" Mutt cried angrily. "You go into a little slump and talk about quitting? Where's your guts?"

"But, Pa—"

"Slumps happen to everybody. But you can't give in to 'em, you hear? You get back in there and play ball. That's all there is for you, unless you want to spend your life grubbing in the mines like me. Well? Are you going to quit, or are you going to try?"

Mickey swallowed and wiped his eyes. "I'll try," he said.

Back with the team, Mickey *(center)* jumps for joy as Joe DiMaggio *(5)* comes home to score on a safe bunt by Phil Rizzuto.

Mickey said later that the bawling out was the finest thing his father had ever done for him. It gave him the courage to stop feeling sorry for himself.

He snapped out of the slump the next day. After 35 games, his average was back up to .360.

Casey Stengel called him up. "Okay, kid, come on back," he said. Mickey rejoined the Yankees at the end of August.

This time it was for keeps.

The Yankees were locked in a pennant race with the Cleveland Indians and needed all the help they could get. Mickey showed them what he could do by slugging a two-run homer the first time at bat.

In those last crucial weeks, he delivered in the clutch and helped his team wrap up first place. He still struck out a lot, however, and Joe DiMaggio had his hands full coaching Mickey in the outfield.

The Yankees faced the New York Giants in a "subway series" in 1951. Mickey was hitless in the first game. The team lost, 5-1.

In the second game, he dragged a bunt. Then Phil Rizzuto bunted and Mickey went to second. Gil McDougald came up next, and his screaming drive sent Mickey home for his first World Series run.

Mutt watched from the stands, his dreams come true.

Mr. and Mrs. Mantle greet Mickey. Behind him is his girl friend, Merlyn Johnson, and his brother Ray.

Mickey falls injured at the feet of Joe DiMaggio.

In the top of the fifth inning, Willie Mays of the Giants hit a high fly. Joe DiMaggio and Mickey went for it. Suddenly Mickey fell to the ground. Joe fielded the ball, then ran to see what had happened.

Mickey had caught his spikes in a drain cover and injured his knee. Next morning, he and Mutt took a taxi to a hospital for x-rays. When Mutt tried to help his son walk, the older man suddenly fell.

"Pa! What's wrong?" Mickey exclaimed.

It was not until weeks later that Mickey found out that Mutt had cancer. Mickey's injuries healed, but his father died the next spring.

30

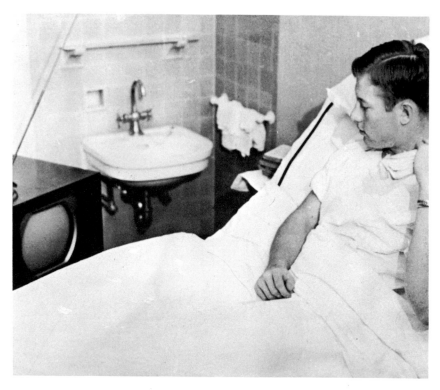

Mickey and his father, hospitalized together, watched the rest of the 1951 World Series on television.

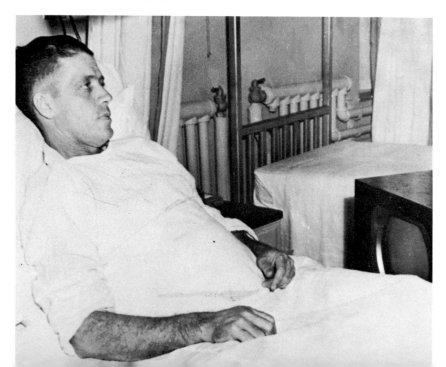

Late in 1951, Mickey and Merlyn Johnson were married. She helped cheer him during Mutt's last illness.

Despite his sorrow, Mickey worked hard to get his leg in shape for the 1952 season. He was still limping in April, and Yankee fans were in a grim mood. The immortal Joe DiMaggio had finally retired. Three other top players were lost to the army draft. A lot—maybe too much—was going to depend on a green kid named Mickey Mantle. His leg injuries had made him 4-F, an army reject.

Mickey scores the tying run in the fourth inning of the second game of the 1952 World Series. Waiting for the ball is Brooklyn Dodger catcher Roy Campanella. The Yankees won, 7-1.

The fans began booing Mickey louder than ever. He had a good season at bat—despite the fact that he led the league in strikeouts. The Yankees clinched still another pennant—their fourth in a row—when Mickey homered against Philadelphia. He got two homers in the World Series, too, and the Yankees won.

Still, Mickey was booed more than any other player in big-league history.

After striking out, Mickey flips his bat in disgust.

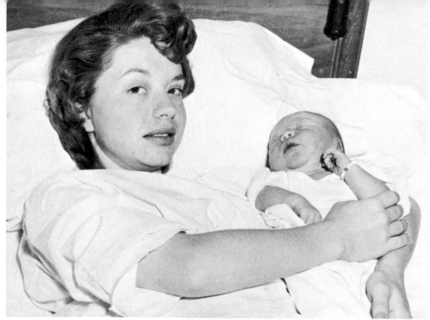

Merlyn holds the Mantles' firstborn son, Mickey Elven.

He tried not to let the fans get him down. Some resented him because they thought he was trying to fill the shoes of the beloved DiMaggio. Others thought he was a poor sport because he showed his anger when he struck out. They even called him a draft-dodger.

Mickey closed his ears and kept on slugging.

He started the next season with a bombshell. On April 17, 1953, in Washington's Griffith Stadium, he came to bat in the fifth with one man on. The Yanks led, 2-1.

Batting right-handed against a southpaw pitcher, he let the first ball go by. He connected with the next.

The ball flew upward, over the center-field bleachers, 55 feet high. It bounced off a sign and a roof and finally rested in a back yard, where a small boy found it.

It had gone 565 feet, the longest homer in history.

After that, there was always a fellow busy with a tape measure. Mickey slugged a 420-footer in Yankee Stadium, a 485-footer in St. Louis, and sent the ball 425 feet in Chicago. The sportswriters began to put him right up there with the great hitters of all time—Babe Ruth, Lou Gehrig, and Jimmy Foxx.

Before each game, he had to tape his injured legs to strengthen them. But he streaked down the base paths like a comet, and his fielding was becoming very good indeed.

And still the fans booed him.

In mid-season, hard luck struck Mickey again. He pulled a thigh muscle. A few weeks later he hurt his knee again and was benched for part of the time.

Wrapping his legs was a constant pre-game chore for Mickey.

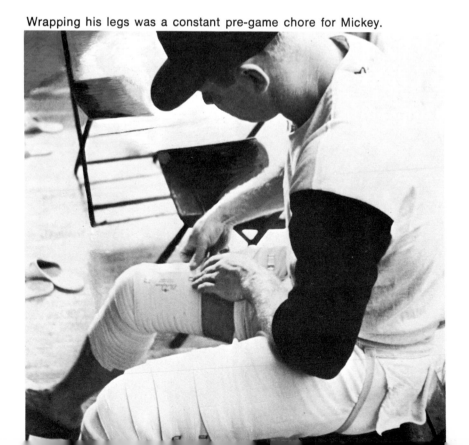

Despite this, the Yanks took the pennant again. But Mickey, weakened and in constant pain, could not fulfill the promise of earlier months. His excellent early batting average sank to .296 by the end of the season.

There was still the World Series. Mickey hobbled to the plate 25 times and managed only five hits. But he earned his pay. One hit was a two-run homer. Another was a glorious grand-slam home run that gave the Yankees the championship over the Brooklyn Dodgers.

It took two operations to put Mickey's knee back into some sort of shape for the 1954 season. But this wasn't going to be a memorable year for him, nor for the Yanks either.

Congratulations are in order as Mickey hits the fourth grand slam homer in World Series history, October 4, 1953. Mickey's teammates are Joe Collins, Hank Bauer and Yogi Berra. In background are Dodger catcher Roy Campanella and umpire Bill Grieve.

The team came in second. Mickey came in first—as strikeout king. Writers said that they were "disappointed" that he had not done better, even though he had led the league in runs scored. The fans kept on booing.

It had become a fad to boo Mickey Mantle. They kept it up during the next four years, when the Yankees won four pennants and two World Series.

The years 1955-1958 saw Mickey become one of the top players in baseball. He was home-run champ in 1955, 1956, and 1958. He led the league in runs scored in 1956, 1957, and 1958. In 1956 he also led in runs batted in, giving him baseball's coveted Triple Crown, last won in 1947 by Ted Williams of Boston.

He was voted Most Valuable Player in 1956 and 1957. His salary soared.

Casey Stengel crowns King Mickey with baseball's Triple Crown. He closed the 1956 season with a batting average of .353, 52 homers and 130 runs batted in.

After being struck out three times, Mickey complains to umpire Joe Paparella. Mickey's bat lies on the ground.

Then came more injuries to his legs and shoulder. He did not snap back as quickly as he had when he was younger. Instead, pain and stiffness weakened his swing in late 1958 and 1959. He fell into another slump.

Mickey himself has said that 1959 was his worst year. His performance was bad, his attitude on the field worse. He was impatient and disgusted because he could not do better. He lost confidence.

The team came in third that fall. Nearly everyone seemed to think it was Mickey's fault, even though the rest of the ball club certainly shared the blame. The Yankee management made Mickey take a salary cut.

The first two months of the 1960 season were blackest of all. The Yankees lost 20 games out of 40. Young fans mobbed and punched Mickey. He had hit rock bottom in his relations with the fans.

Mickey's pride was deeply hurt. He brooded and became careless. The team fought valiantly to regain first place in the American League. They were sparked by a bright new hitter, Roger Maris.

But Mickey didn't seem to care any more. One day in August, he came to bat with Maris on first, the score tied at 1-1, and one out. Mickey hit a ground ball toward third base.

It was easily scooped up and fired to second, where Maris was sliding in, cracking a couple of ribs as he did.

Casey Stengel poses with members of his 1960 ball club. From left to right they are: Roger Maris, Yogi Berra, Mickey Mantle, Bobby Richardson, Bill Skowron, Tony Kubek, Art Ditmar, Hector Lopez, Cletis Boyer.

With Mickey up to bat, Roger Maris *(left)* leads away from first.

The fans let out an unbelieving howl. Mickey had simply turned from the plate and walked toward the dugout! Why hadn't he run?

He had thought there were two outs instead of one.

Casey Stengel threw Mickey out of the game. When Mickey realized what he had done, he hated himself. Sunk in misery back in the clubhouse, he was sure that the team and the fans must hate him too.

But they didn't. To his surprise, fellow-Yankees told him not to worry. They said they had made the same kind of mistakes themselves. As the others tried to make him feel better, a truth came home to Mickey.

He had been thinking only of his own performance, and not of the good of the team. He had let the rest of them down.

41

Mickey resolved that he would never let it happen again.

"From now on," he told himself, "I'm putting out one hundred per cent. All the time."

It was like a curtain going up on a new life. The next day, Mickey began breaking out of his slump. The Yanks met the Baltimore Orioles. In the fourth inning, the Orioles led, 2-0. There was a man on first as Mickey came to the plate.

He stood there full of confidence again. The ball flew in and he swung. *Crack!* The fans had something to scream about as the ball went 400 feet into the bullpen for a homer.

The score was tied.

Next time up, Mickey popped out. The Orioles scored again. At bat once more, with two strikes against him, Mickey sent the ball winging into the stands to win the ball game. He trotted around the bases, and coming home, he tipped his hat to the fans.

Suddenly, they loved him.

Mickey's face shows concentration as he practices batting.

No other baseball star was as injury-plagued as Mickey Mantle. The picture, taken in 1963, points out only a few of his disabilities. From head to toe: tonsillectomy, 1956; injured right shoulder, 1957; rib injury, 1963; hip abscess, 1961; broken finger, 1959; pulled thigh muscle, 1955 and 1962; knee cyst, 1954; sprained knee, 1956; injured knee, 1962; knee operations, 1951 and 1952; osteomyelitis, before 1947; and broken foot, 1963.

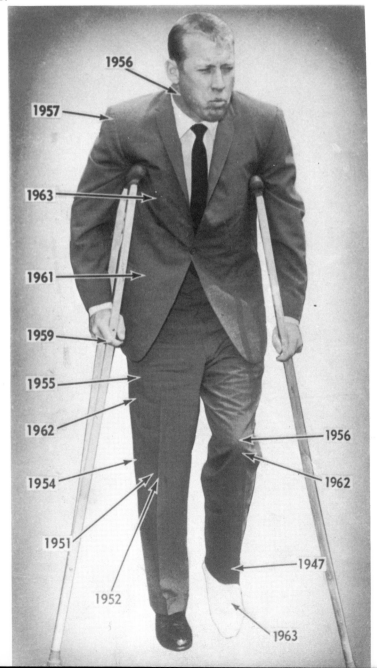

Mickey blasts a home run in the fourth inning of the third game in the
1960 World Series.

Young fans and old greet Mickey at Yankee Stadium.

Mickey Mantle and Roger Maris pose together in 1961.

The Yankees regained first place and went straight to a pennant. The World Series was lost to Pittsburgh by a single clutch home run. Mickey wept after that heartbreaker. The fans warmed to him more than ever.

Roger Maris, the marvelous new Yankee slugger, took some of the pressure off Mickey. In 1961 they had a goodnatured "duel" trying to break Babe Ruth's home-run record of 60 in one season. Mickey was also appointed "team leader" by the new manager, Ralph Houk. As he worked to keep up the fighting spirit of the other Yankees, Mickey was able to forget his own troubles.

The 1961 season ended with Roger Maris breaking Ruth's record, set in 1927. Roger had 61 home runs, Mickey 54.

No one cheered louder than Mickey when Roger won the Most Valuable Player award.

Three of the world's top home run hitters came together in 1969. From left: Willie Mays, Mickey Mantle, Hank Aaron.

The next year, it was Mickey's turn to win it—for the third time. He suffered several injuries and missed 47 games. But he kept coming back to inspire the team and to wallop the ball.

The Yankees wrapped up another pennant race and World Series. Mickey topped the league in slugging.

People remembered him standing fast at the plate in spite of the pain, limping around the bases, refusing to stay benched because he wanted to be out there with the team.

They agreed that he deserved the Most Valuable Player award. For performance? Yes, he had played well.

But more than that, the award had honored his courage. For this was what had made Mickey Mantle truly great.

46

MICKEY CHARLES MANTLE

He was born October 20, 1931, in the northeastern Oklahoma town of Spavinaw. His father, Elven "Mutt" Mantle, was a keen amateur baseball player. From the first, Mutt set out to make his son a top slugger. Because of his teaching, Mickey became the greatest switch hitter in history.

Mickey married Merlyn Louise Johnson, his high-school sweetheart, on December 23, 1951. The couple had four sons. After a boyhood of poverty, Mickey became a wealthy man through his sports career and business investments.

He played for the Yankees from 1951 until 1968, when pain from his innumerable injuries finally forced his retirement. Despite his disabilities, he was one of the top hitters of all time. His lifetime home run record was 536, number four after Babe Ruth, Willie Mays, and Hank Aaron. He is also the lifetime strikeout king with a total of 1,710. His record of the longest home run (565 feet) still stands, and the ball is enshrined at Baseball's Hall of Fame in Coopertown, N.Y.

Mickey has written an autobiography, *The Education of a Baseball Player*.

MICKEY MANTLE STATISTICS

Year	Club	G	AB	R	H	2B	3B	HR	RBI	SO	BA
1949	Independence	89	323	54	101	15	7	7	63	66	.313
1950	Joplin	137	519	141	199	30	12	26	136	90	.383
1951	New York	96	341	61	91	11	5	13	65	74	.267
	Kansas City	40	166	32	60	9	3	11	50	30	.361
1952	New York	142	549	94	171	37	7	23	87	*111	.311
1953	New York	127	461	105	136	24	3	21	92	90	.295
1954	New York	146	543	*129	163	17	12	27	102	*107	.300
1955	New York	147	517	121	158	25	*11	*37	99	97	.306
1956	New York	150	533	*132	188	22	5	*52	*130	99	*.353
1957	New York	144	474	*121	173	28	6	34	94	75	.365
1958	New York	150	519	*127	158	21	1	*42	97	*120	.304
1959	New York	144	541	104	154	23	4	31	75	*126	.285
1960	New York	153	527	*119	145	17	6	*40	94	*125	.275
1961	New York	153	514	*132	163	16	6	54	128	112	.317
1962	New York	123	377	96	121	15	1	30	89	78	.321
1963	New York	65	172	40	54	8	0	15	35	32	.314
1964	New York	143	465	92	141	25	2	35	111	102	.303
1965	New York	122	361	44	92	12	1	19	46	76	.255
1966	New York	108	333	40	96	12	1	23	56	76	.288
1967	New York	144	440	63	108	17	0	22	55	113	.245
1968	New York	144	435	57	103	14	1	18	54	97	.237
Major League Totals		2401	8102	1677	2415	344	72	536	1509	*1710	.298

*League leader

Leading Player in World Series

Most runs scored, total series: 42
Most runs batted in, total series: 40
Most home runs, total series: 18
Most total bases, total series: 123
Most bases on balls, total series: 43
Most strikeouts, total series: 54

Most Valuable Player Award
1956
1957
1962